ADVENTURING FOR CHRISTIAN UNITY:

A Survey of the History of Churches of Christ (Disciples)

by

DEAN E. WALKER, M.A., B.D.

(Professor of Church History, School of Religion, Butler University, Indianapolis, Indiana, U.S.A.)

with a Foreword by

W. ROBINSON, M.A.

(Principal, Overdale College, and Lecturer in Christian Doctrine and the Philosophy of Religion, Selly Oak Colleges).

1935.

Printed in England

CONTENTS.

		Page
FOREWORD	. . . .	5
INTRODUCTION	. . . .	13

CHAPTER I.

| FROM REFORMATION TO RESTORATION: 1793 TO 1835 | . . . . | 17 |

CHAPTER II.

| RESTORATION AT WORK: 1835 TO 1930 | . . | 35 |

FOREWORD.*

THERE is a strange contradiction observed in the writings of St. Paul, which to little minds who dearly love consistency is very embarrassing. It is the double emphasis on *liberty* and on *order*. Sometimes the great apostle seems to be an arrant individualist, and at other times a convinced institutionalist. It is chiefly in his earlier epistles —Romans and Galatians—that the former attitude is stressed, and in his later epistles—Colossians and Ephesians—that the latter attitude finds clearest expression. So conflicting do the two attitudes seem to be on a cursory reading, that early New Testament critics declared that the two sets of writings could not have come from the same man (a position which is now no longer held by sane critics, and one which was based on a too narrow ideal of consistency, as well as on a faulty psychological insight).

But all down the ages the contradiction has given rise to varying estimates of Paul, best illustrated by two modern Protestant writers. Professor C. H. Dodd of Manchester finds in Paul the champion of those who can never satisfy themselves with institutional religion ; while Bousset, a great continental scholar, thought of Paul as the very founder of Christian institutionalism ! Undoubtedly in Paul there are to be found both the emphasis on liberty and the emphasis on authority in a certain sense.

But the trouble is that all down the ages Paul has been largely misunderstood so far as his doctrine of the Church is concerned. We have only to read the works of his immediate successors, such as Clement of Rome, Ignatius, and Justin Martyr, to see how very far the spiritual thermometer, which stands so high in the Pauline writings, had really fallen a generation or two later. In their literal sense the words of Paul might be honoured, but in their true spiritual meaning they were little understood. It is true, as George Eliot

---

* The substance of this Foreword is reprinted from the *Christian Union Quarterly for* July, 1929.

5

has said, that we never really understand the words of a truly great man until we have learned to share, in some measure, the experiences out of which they grew.

This is nowhere better illustrated than in the writings of the second century, which seek to interpret for the Church the mind of Paul. It was one thing for *Paul* to speak of " coming with a rod," but it is quite another thing—and a dangerous thing—for lesser men than Paul to follow his example. By the close of the second century, especially in the West, the Church had—largely due to the pressure of heretical sects, but partly because there were no minds big enough to grasp the true essentials in Paul's teaching— become thoroughly legalised and defended by rigid bulwarks of creed, sacred canon of Scripture, and ordered hierarchy of ministry. So the unity of the institution was safeguarded, and within the next four centuries—again under the pressure of heresy—all this was crystallising and hardening, until it appears in the fully developed Roman system, with its centralised organ of authority.

Yet, for another thousand years, there was some measure of liberty, and the Popes were by no means masters in their own house. The Middle Ages, with their theological and philosophical disputants, are sufficient witness to this. The Reformation, however, further helped the hardening process, and from this experience Rome emerged—in reaction to what she regarded as Protestant heresies— as a closed system, an institution wherein was the minimum of liberty in the realms of thought and morality. Rome was hence- forth—if she thought at all—to think corporately, not in the sense which Paul had stressed of each member contributing to the corporate result, but in the sense that she was to have a special organ of thought—the infallible Pope (really and truly the Roman curia). This, in effect, meant that she was, in the main, to think in a circle. This is not to say that there have not been great thinkers in the Roman communion—one remembers with gratitude the Baron von Hügel—but the position of such thinkers has always been precarious, as was illustrated in the cases of Tyrrell and Loisy.

Now the Protestant Churches at the Reformation largely followed the example of Rome, and sought to preserve their unity by a legalised interpretation of Christianity, set forth in various creeds and confessions like those of Westminster, Augsburg, and the Thirty-nine Articles. Erasmus, though he remained a faithful son of Rome, had warned men in his day that " by identifying the new learning with heresy, you make orthodoxy synonymous with ignorance " ; but in spite of this warning the creed makers of the sixteenth and early seventeenth centuries pursued their task of interpreting the Christian facts in the thought terms of their own day, and thus largely denied to the Church of the future the right to think outside these categories.

But all this ultra-institutionalism is a misunderstanding of Paul's thought, and of the fundamental nature of personality too, especially as regards corporate relationships. Paul is neither a libertarian, in the sense of advocating complete freedom of thought and action for every individual, nor is he a rigid institutionalist, in the sense of regarding the Church as a mechanical thing with rules and regulations of a legalised nature. Laws there may be, but they are not of the arbitrary kind. They are the kind of laws *which are fundamental to personality itself* in its human relationships. Such is the law of love. Paul's view of the Church is that of an organism—not a machine—a body, capable of growth and development. It is that of a *fellowship* society—a Divine Society ; for, let it be said, Paul's view is a *high* view—whose keynote is *corporate loyalty*, and not legalised discipline ; whose bond is love and not authority in the usually accepted sense. Those who rule are, indeed, those who *have become the bondslaves of all*. Individualism—where every man is a law unto himself, and every immature thinker is a prophet selling new lamps for old, and asserting that " he speaks in the name of the morality of the future," when, indeed, he has neither experience of life nor understanding—may, indeed, be a truly ugly thing, perhaps far more ugly than a regimented, legalised, authoritarian institutionalism. But St. Paul's thought had room for neither. He saw in a religion which *based itself on personality*—

7

for such was Christianity—the possibility of a Church which transcended both—at once the home of freedom and of loyalty. For the soul needs both freedom and loyalty for its highest development. In fact, freedom is loyalty, and loyalty is freedom. He is most free who is most loyal, providing he chooses a loyalty which is big enough for freedom to develop in, and so further deepen his loyalty. In other words, loyalty is the only atmosphere in which freedom can work. As Josiah Royce said, "In loyalty, when loyalty is properly defined, is the fulfilment of the whole moral law."

It was in the early years of the nineteenth century, when Christianity in all its forms was thoroughly creed-bound and legalised in its expression (apart from Quakers and Unitarians, though Unitarians often had a rigid negative creed), or on the other hand was thoroughly anarchical in the strange sects which multiplied, that a Movement began simultaneously in America and the British Isles. This Movement set itself the paradoxical task of freeing the Church from legalistic and authoritarian institutionalism on the one hand, and from anarchical individualism on the other. It had for its prophets such men as William Jones, M.A., of London, and Alexander Campbell, Walter Scott, and Barton W. Stone in America. It was finally forced, against its will, into denominational expression, and is represented to-day by Disciples in America and by Churches of Christ in Great Britain and her colonies.

Now Churches of Christ (Disciples) have ever pleaded for the unity of the Church, but they have preferred to rest their whole case for unity on the Pauline basis of liberty and corporate loyalty. They have not felt that loyalty is best preserved in the Body by legalised methods of setting up infallible standards in credalised forms. They have preferred to walk within a garden without such clearly defined fences, one which might even open on to the moors and waste places; knowing that, should any stray out into the wild, hunger would bring them back to the plentifully supplied garden, and that the loss of colour and scent, which, once in the waste places,

was theirs no longer, would produce its own heartache and consequent retracing of their footsteps. Or to change the metaphor
they have preferred to ask Christians to live dangerously, and so
they have demanded of those who came to Baptism, no assent
to written creeds enshrining theological dogmas, but simply an
oath of allegiance to Jesus as Lord.

They have sought to secure a *personal* basis for love working
itself out in loyalty to Jesus and to the corporate society which is
His Body, the Church ; and to stress the fact that to be a traitor
to such a loyalty, based and founded in love, is a more heinous
sin than to be a little muddle-headed on some theological explanation of a fact of experience. Like Father Tyrrell, the founders of the
Movement made a distinction between " dogma " as a fact of
Christian experience, and " theology " as an explanation of
Christian facts in language suited to the thought of a single age.
And it is a striking testimony to the value of this distinction that
the great Christian facts of the Fatherhood of God, the Deity and
perfect Humanity of Jesus Christ, His redeeming work for mankind,
and the indwelling of the Holy Spirit have been tenaciously held
without theological creeds playing any part at all in conserving
unity. As in the early Church, the unity has been a unity of life
based upon a mystical experience of these great facts of our common
faith. Churches of Christ use only the baptismal confession, " I
believe that Jesus is the Christ, the Son of the Living God," which
makes the Person of Jesus central and is really an *oath of allegiance*
to Him. That, in preserving the unity of the Faith, they have been
helped by their emphasis on Baptism and the Lord's Supper—
their loyalty to these two sacraments, and to the idea of the one
Body—there can be little doubt ; for dogma is best enshrined in
dramatic form, better transmitted by art than by logical definition.

All this, of course, has not always been equally well maintained.
The early teachers a century ago had few or no followers of equal
intellectual grasp, and certainly few of the same spiritual stature.
There were many who sought to set up unwritten creeds more

rigid in their demands than written ones. Sometimes they have seemed even to dominate the Churches and to cramp their life and imprison it within the narrowest possible compass, hedging it round by infallible barriers as rigid as those of Rome. But such have never understood the real genius of the Movement to which they have belonged, and, so far as I know, have never succeeded in gaining a single conviction for heresy, largely because, on a basis of liberty and a free fellowship in love, corporate loyalty has been maintained at a maximum and real heresies have not appeared. And, further, on the truly personal basis of liberty and corporate loyalty, whilst there will be no sympathy with opinions which definitely undermine Christian faith and morals, it will be realised that any real authority which can deal with their rejection must depend upon a free and not a managed consensus.

I trust that no one will conclude that this is written in disparagement of theology, nor in disparagement of any adequate philosophy of the Christian Faith. Quite the opposite is the case. There must be within the Church the fullest room for theological and philosophical advancement, and a community which dares to found itself on the principle of an instructed Church membership rather than on the principle of a sacerdotally guided or dogmatically guided membership must, more than any other, give attention to scholarship. But just for this very reason the Church must not lend herself to, nor base her unity upon, the philosophy or theology of any one age. She must base it on something deeper and more abiding. Neither do I wish to deny that creeds—statements of Christian belief—may have their use and have had all down the ages, some being much more permanent than others. But they have been permanent in the degree in which they have confined themselves to "dogma" in Tyrrell's sense, rather than to "theology," and, in any case, they are not the best safeguards of the Church's unity. They have their limits. But the oath of *loyalty* has no such limits. To take Him as both Lord and Christ is to set out on a task which can find its consummation only when we reach Him and are like Him—when we see Him as He is.

Professor Dean Walker has written an admirable account of the history of the Movement in America. Its line of descent in this country was through the Glasites and Sandemanians via the Haldanes and the Scotch Baptists, to all of whom Alexander Campbell was much indebted. From about 1830 the two Movements, here and in America, were in association. Although there was no *world* organisation until 1930, and development proceeded unhindered except by personal contacts and interchange of literature, there has been no drifting apart. Development in both countries has been along similar lines.* Here, growth has been by no means so rapid as in America. Old-established traditions have had to be overcome. There are, however, some 200 churches in Great Britain, and from here the Movement has spread to Australia, New Zealand, Canada, and South Africa. Churches of Christ in Great Britain maintain mission stations in Siam, India, and Central Africa. Altogether, Churches of Christ are represented in some thirty-five countries by over two million members. The first World Convention was held in Washington, D.C., in 1930, and the second is to be held in Leicester this year.†

Professor Walker has produced a brilliant study of the ideals and motives which inspired the pioneers over a century ago, and a living picture of how these ideals were worked out. The double passion for the unity of the Church universal and the minimising of credal elements, which he so ably describes, has lived with us throughout our short history, and will live until we all come to the unity of the Faith in the bonds of peace. I count it a joy and a privilege to be asked to write a Foreword to this survey which he first delivered as lectures in the Summer School of Overdale College in 1934. Professor Walker has done a double service. For

* This is here amply illustrated. The brief interpretation of the Movement which I give in this Foreword was written six years ago, but *had never been read* by Professor Walker until it appeared here. Readers will appreciate that the two interpretations are almost identical.

† For a fuller account of the history, faith, and practice of Churches of Christ, see my book *What Churches of Christ Stand For*, *Discipleship in the Church*, by James Gray, M.A., and *Convictions*, edited by Canon L. Hodgson.

those outside the Movement he has provided a brilliant interpretation of its aims and ideals ; and for Disciples everywhere he has drawn a picture which ought to thrill them with a sense of their glorious heritage, and inspire them to a new loyalty and courage.

W. ROBINSON.

OVERDALE COLLEGE,
SELLY OAK,
BIRMINGHAM.

INTRODUCTION.

THE problem of Christian unity is to-day shifting from the realm of academic discussion to that of practical policy. The history of one of the earliest of such practical movements is therefore of significance. That Movement, known variously as Disciples of Christ and Churches of Christ, is now well into its second century. Not only does it claim to propose a plan of Reunion, but it urges that it has engaged upon the practice of it. As its second World Convention gathers in Leicester this summer (1935), a brief presentation of its history may not be inappropriate. This history in itself may be a contribution to the solution of the problem of a divided Church.

Disciples, however, do not limit the application of their position to this problem. They deplore the tendency of practical Church life to cling to things long declared by theological science to be indifferent. They insist that the communal and sacramental life of the Church must have the same moral grounding as that of individual responsibility. They plead that the practical re-integration of the Church is a necessary prelude to the unification of mankind. They hold that this re-integration is at once ethical and mystical, and involves a reconsideration of the nature and functions of evangelism, conversion, and corporate communal life. They point to the original confession of the Lordship of Christ as embodying the essential ground of creed and authority in religion. They appeal to the common Christian mind, through the qualified scholarship and piety of the Church Catholic, in problems of interpretation of revelation.

How far does the history of this particular people exemplify these ideals? They do not claim to have achieved perfection. But it may reasonably be said that their history does not invalidate their claims. This fact may be illustrated by the diversity of external practice existing between the Churches in Britain and those in

America. A casual examination notes striking differences. A closer acquaintance reveals that these differences are the accidents of cultural environment. An intimate study discloses in both groups of Churches the same temper of spirit, the same outlook on religious and social questions, and the same ultimate reliances. That this should be the case, in spite of somewhat different origins, and of independent development, is a significant commentary on the catholic nature of " the plea."

The two lectures herein presented comprise a study of the American phase of the Movement. Unfortunately, I have not been able to document them suitably, although their popular nature somewhat excuses the lack. They are based on a fairly extensive study of the literature of the Disciples. There is no comprehensive history of the Movement. This is due in some measure to the lack of a sufficient number of local studies. The deficiency seems about to be removed, especially in view of such pioneer works as that of Dr. Garrison's *Religion Follows the Frontier* (1931). For the present work I must content myself by acknowledging my deep debt to my former teacher, Dean F. D. Kershner, of the College of Religion, Butler University, for his analysis of the *Declaration and Address* in his *Christian Union Overture*, which I have adopted with some modification.

The lectures are presented, without revision, as prepared and delivered through the courtesy of Principal Robinson and the Governors of Overdale College, during the summer of 1934. I am indebted to them, and to Mrs. Robinson, for the generous facilities afforded at that time. By the further interest of the Principal, and the Publishing Committee of Churches of Christ in Great Britain, these studies are now made available in their present form.

The development of the Movement in Britain is not less important than in America. The variations are themselves indicative of applications to which each group should attend. It is to be regretted that Mr. Robinson has had to limit himself to a brief Foreword, which, however, in a remarkable way, illustrates the

14

unity of the British and American Churches and the workableness of " the plea " advanced by Churches of Christ. He has written elsewhere a brief introduction to the history of the Movement in this country,* and this should be read along with my own brief survey. The literature of the Movement in Britain awaits an adequate survey before a representative history can be written. It is to be hoped that such work will not be long in appearing. And when it does, it will be indebted to Principal Robinson for the present Foreword and what he has written elsewhere.

DEAN E. WALKER.

EDINBURGH.
January, 1935.

---

* See *What Churches of Christ Stand For*.

CHAPTER I

FROM REFORMATION TO RESTORATION: 1793 TO 1835.

THE Restoration Movement in America is a confluence of six streams of Christian action. These are, in origin, quite distinct. Arising simultaneously, they discovered each other and clarified their objectives within a generation. The story of the beginnings is therefore necessarily scattered at first, but unifies toward the fourth decade of the nineteenth century.

I.—BEGINNINGS: 1793 TO 1813.

By the close of the Revolutionary War, the Wesleyans in the United States had gained independence from both the Anglican Church and the Wesleyan superintendency. When Asbury, commissioned by Wesley to re-establish his supremacy, assumed Episcopal functions on the 25th December, 1793, he met with considerable opposition, headed by James O'Kelly. Termed at first " Republican Methodist," Rice Haggard suggested in 1794 that " henceforth the followers of Christ be known as Christians simply," and A. M. Hafferty moved that the Bible itself be taken as their only creed. Both motions were accepted, and the first church was established at Chapel Hill, N.C., the site of the University. Inheriting the Methodist enthusiasm for evangelism, the Movement made rapid strides, especially in rural Virginia and the Carolinas. Many of these Christians soon moved westward, founding other pioneer churches, or lying dormant until the awakening of religion on the frontier. In general, they followed the orthodox evangelicalism of the day, but were characterised by an independence and freedom of spirit quite foreign to the imported European denominations.

In 1800 Abner Jones left the Free Will Baptists to organise an independent church at Lyndon, N.H., whose members assumed the name of Christian only, discarding all human creeds. Assisted by Elias Smith, he travelled throughout New England and Eastern Canada, making many converts. A religious newspaper was founded in 1805, *The Herald of Gospel Liberty*, which exerted much influence until 1930, when it was merged with *The Congregationalist*. With true catholicity this body of people refused to be bound by traditional theology, though retaining largely the mystical conception of conversion so prevalent in America after Jonathan Edwards. They also contributed largely to the westward migration following the Revolution, especially to Ohio.

The vices of frontier life, drunkenness, gambling, and fighting, greatly shocked the Presbyterian ministers who came west with the people. Among them was Barton Warren Stone, born in 1772, a descendant of a Governor of provincial Maryland. Educated at Guildford Academy, he was ordained in 1798 by the Transylvania Presbytery, in spite of agreeing to the Westminster Confession only " so far as consistent with the word of God." Assigned to the Cane Ridge Church, Stone instituted in 1801 a revival which is famed as the most extensive in America. He was assisted by Methodist and Baptist preachers. Over 30,000 people congregated at one time. They came from hundreds of miles, on foot, horseback, and in wagons. The attention of the world was drawn to this revival.

Most people seemed chiefly interested in the physical phenomena attending the preaching—the jerks, the barks, and the like. But Stone deprecated them as evidences of conversion, although not denying that they might be the signs of the working of the Holy Spirit. That in the camp meeting which caught his attention, and which proved to have lasting results, was the preaching and the change in the people attending. Without any mutual agreement, the preachers of all denominations were neglecting their peculiarities of credal expression, and speaking in Biblical terms. The note of warning against sin was strong ; but the note of God's love for mankind was stronger. Responding, people, regardless of creed, united in prayer and in Communion. In professing conversion, no one obtruded the symbolical standards* as a pre-requisite to admission to the church. To all those participating it seemed that the day of religious animosity had gone.

Scarcely had the crowds departed, leaving Cane Ridge and all other churches in Kentucky much stronger, when the various denominational heads descended to rebuild the fences. Stone was accused of departing from Calvinism. Together with four other Presbyterian preachers, he withdrew from the Synod, and formed an independent Presbytery in 1803. This manœuvre spared him a heresy trial, but did not increase his love of Presbyterianism. He issued his first book, *The Apology of the Springfield Presbytery*, which is a severe indictment of Confessions as bonds of communion. " The Bible alone is our rule of faith and practice," he says, defining the position of the defiant Presbytery.

But during the revival a new passion had been aroused in Stone—an intense longing for Christian union. Even so liberal a

---

*The expression ' symbolical standards,' with its derivative forms, has reference to the Church creeds.

Presbytery as Springfield was seen to be partisan. So, in June, 1804, this organisation was dissolved, and at the suggestion of Rice Haggard, the reformers assumed the name of Christian simply. The occasion was signalised by the publication of *The Last Will and Testament of the Springfield Presbytery*. Cast in a rather satirical tone, this document demands the death of denominationalism in the interest of union ; denies the distinction between clergy and laity ; repudiates the power of synods to legislate for government of the Church ; asserts the mystical selection of preachers by the Holy Spirit ; calls for congregational government but provides for strong co-operation in matters of mutual interest ; and urges universal application to Bible study, pointing out the individual responsibility of all men thereto.

The document is obviously a product of the hour. But so was the Movement inaugurated in the Cane Ridge Revival. It caught the popular fancy. It was not burdened with theology. It was democratic. It rejoiced in Christian fellowship. It stressed the love of God. It thrived on the contrite sorrow for sin evidenced at the mourner's bench and leading to an ethical change in life. It was the religious salvation of the new West.

Indiana is in many respects the heart of America. Into this State poured all the streams of migration westward. Each new group brought its church. In 1810 John Wright organised a Free Baptist Church, but adopted no articles of faith. In 1813 an association of Free Baptist Churches was formed, which soon dropped the name Baptist, and adopted the Bible as their creed " without note or comment." The next year they dissolved the association into an Annual Meeting. Then they entered into discussion with fifteen German Baptists (Tunkers) and came to an agreement. This united body then united with the New Lights, as the followers of Stone were called. Meanwhile, the Silver Creek Baptist Association had become saturated with the teachings of Alexander Campbell, and a further union was formed with this group. By 1820 these " Churches of Christ " embraced a membership rivalling the Methodists, supported by their eastern mission board. This Movement, in which Wright was the leader, is significant for many reasons, among which not the least is its anticipation of the events of 1832, or the consolidation of the Restoration Movement.

Between 1800 and 1820 large numbers of Scotsmen arrived in America. Among them were many from the various independent religious bodies of Scotland and Ireland. By 1816 Scotch Baptists had founded churches in New York, Baltimore, Philadelphia,

Danbury (Conn.), Pittsburgh, and elsewhere. I need not speak here concerning the devotion of these people to the Bible, nor of their earnest search for an exact pattern of Church government found therein.

The Scotch Baptists were not zealous evangelists, but rather careful students of Church order. Burdened by a severe Calvinism, they were, perhaps, not over-anxious to grow rapidly. None the less, their influence was far beyond their numbers. Three of the greatest men of the Movement in America came through them—Walter Scott, Dr. Robert Richardson, and Isaac Errett. And as we shall have occasion to see, their tight, logical thinking has contributed in no small degree to the characteristics of the Disciples throughout their history.

The beginnings of the sixth of these streams, that of the Campbells, is of vital importance. In 1804, the year Stone became a Christian only, dissolving his Presbyterianism, Thomas Campbell attempted to unite the Burghers and anti-Burghers in Ireland. The Irish were willing but the Scots were not, so he failed. But he continued his efforts until his removal to America, where he became minister of a western Presbyterian church near Pittsburgh in 1807. Soon after his arrival he was disciplined by his Presbytery for admitting other Presbyterians than Seceders to Communion. Rather than submit to this limitation of Christian freedom and fraternity, he withdrew from the Presbytery, but not from the Church, and formed "The Christian Association of Washington." The design of this group was not to form a new church, but to agitate Presbyterians and others on the question of creeds. He was at this time a thorough-going Protestant, interested only in the union of Protestants.

In order to put the purpose of the Association before the public, he was commissioned to write a declaration of its aims. This he did, publishing in 1809 the famous *Declaration and Address*,* which was just coming through the press when Alexander Campbell arrived to join his father. Strangely enough the son had reached the same point in his religious development as had the father.

The *Declaration and Address* was over a century before its time. It repays our careful study to-day. Campbell here lays down a platform for Christian union, consisting of thirteen propositions, which may be condensed into five :

* An actual copy of the " page proof " of the *Declaration and Address* is to be found in the Library of Overdale College.

(1) The essential, intentional, and constitutional unity of the Church of Christ. Essential — a divided Church is a self-contradiction. It should be noted at this point that this position is not Protestant, but Catholic, or High Church. Intentional—the Church possesses a divine norm given by its Founder, and schism is sin. Constitutional—the Church's organisation is unitary in its very structure. This unity is to consist (Prop. 2) of the possession by each Christian of the mind of Christ, dominated by the will of Christ, and exhibited in fellowship individually and congregationally. In other words, unity consists not in mere co-operation in service, but in rational agreement on things essential ; while each individual does the work for which his talents fit him, the combined labours of all making complete the work of the Body of Christ on earth.

(2) The supreme authority of Scripture, especially the New Testament. If the first proposition be Catholic, this one is the ultimate and radical Protestant contention. Creeds nullify this fundamental Protestant position. The contention for the supremacy of the New Testament over the Old was quite new and unorthodox in Campbell's day. It closed the doors of all churches against him.

(3) The relative value of theology ; and futility of human creeds. Theology is individually good, but its conclusions are not tests of Christian fellowship. Creeds may be valuable, but are not properly terms of communion.

(4) The essential brotherhood of all Christians. In this proposition Campbell is again Catholic—he avoids the Calvinist criterion of election, as determining who is a Christian. But he is not a Roman Catholic—neither does he assign to Baptism the *sine quâ non*. His tests are : faith, set forth in open profession and obedience to Christ, involving Church membership ; and character, or the harmony of deeds with Our Lord's will ; the whole being practically demonstrated in the concrete, living brotherhood of believers.

(5) If human innovations are removed, Christians will find themselves united. That is, divisions in the Church are due to peculiarities. Discard these, and universalities remain. Here, on the broad ground of the universals, both unity and freedom are found. And, to remove these innovations and to discover what are innovations, means, practically, the restoration of the Church pictured in the New Testament.

Such is the programme of the *Declaration and Address*. If we look beneath for its basic principles, we discover two—one the

21

ultimate Protestant basis and the other Catholic, the two being blended into a unity neither Protestant nor Catholic as popularly understood. The first is, the Lutheran contention of private judgment, plus the Chillingworth statement of the Bible and the Bible alone as the religion of Protestants. Protestants have always been troubled by the seeming inconsistency of these two assumptions. The first seems to lead to anarchy ; and the second to legalism. Out of this arose creeds, as an attempt to resolve the difficulty. The trouble was, each man interpreted his creed as he chose, and the matter remained as before Campbell attacks the problem by repudiating creeds and appealing to the infallibility of the universal reason. And here he is on Catholic ground.

The adoption of the Protestant position of private judgment insured the morality of the religious position. The adoption of the Catholic insured the rationality of this same religious position. Scripture is God's revelation of His will for man's salvation. To understand that will, a consensus of *qualified* opinion is all that is necessary. Reason is a gift of God, the means whereby His Word is to be understood. The possibility of such understanding is inherent in the very term, Word of God.

Nor is this a proposal to determine truth by taking a vote on the question. Mere numbers do not constitute infallibility. But a consensus of the majority of honest and intelligent and spiritual scholars does give the verdict of universal reason. Further, this is not a revival of the authority of Œcumenical Councils—for by common consent such councils are not composed of qualified persons. It is an assertion that in religion, revelation, as interpreted by full and honest scholarship, is the last word; and that unity must rest on truth thus arrived at, or be forever despaired of.

More than once, it should be noted, Thomas Campbell uses the expression, " our brethren of all denominations." This should answer the charge often made that the Campbells did not regard members of denominations as Christians. It is an essential of their plea for Christian unity that there should be Christians to unite. Campbell's thesis was that because they are Christians it is sinful for them to be anything else than united.

So revolutionary a proposal was not answered : it was ignored by the Christian world. The Christian Association of Washington, appealing to the clergy to destroy denominationalism, was considered by them an impertinence. The idea was destined to have children, but they were posthumous.

Thomas Campbell, moved by a desire to prevent the formation of another sect, now applied on the 4th of October, 1810, for admission into the Pittsburgh Synod of the Presbyterian Church (U.S.A.). The Synod refused. His esteem of Presbyterian liberality was sadly disappointed. Against his will, he was forced to organise the Association into a Church, which was accomplished in May, 1811.

Immediately the Campbells set to work to embody in the Brush Run Church the principles enunciated in the *Declaration*. The Lord's Supper was observed weekly, as being an " approved precedent " of the New Testament Church. But Joseph Bryant refused to receive Communion, on the ground that he had not been baptized —although he had been voted a member. Nor would Bryant agree to anything but immersion, since this seemed to him the action of Baptism in the Scripture accounts. Hence, on July 4th, 1811, Thomas Campbell immersed the first new member of the Church. This, and other incidents, impressed on the community the conviction that Baptism was of greater importance than they had at first thought. The issue was brought to a climax by the birth of Alexander Campbell's first child. Should it be baptized according to orthodox custom ? The weight of current Protestantism sanctioned infant baptism. Immemorial custom hallowed it. But, applying the principles of the *Declaration*, the question was no longer, " May we safely reject infant baptism as an innovation ? " ; but, " May we omit believers' baptism, which all admit to be divinely commanded ? "

Note again that Alexander Campbell had canvassed this question in an honest attempt to discover the universal Christian mind on the subject. He ordered, and studied, every book written in English and French, advocating infant baptism and affusion. He discovered admissions in every competent scholar that both were innovations. He appealed to the Greek text. And here he was confronted with immersion as implicit in *baptizo* ; and believer's baptism as the only Baptism.

Having thus thoroughly investigated, after a characteristically Scotch deliberation of two years, Alexander Campbell and others were immersed on June 12th, 1812. But, having made up his mind, Campbell now characteristically assigned as his reasons for the act the Scriptural statement that Baptism is unto remission of sins, into the name of the Father, Son, and Holy Spirit, and that obedience assures the candidate of the gift of Holy Spirit. Nor would he submit to immersion in consequence of the usual questions propounded by the Baptists. Rather, he insisted that it follow on his confession that Jesus is the Christ.

Investigation of Baptism had taught Alexander Campbell the meaning of faith. Before this time both Campbells had been searching for the least number of items which men must believe in order to salvation. Thomas Campbell had taught Alexander to apply universal reason to what seemed to his private judgment to be taught in the Bible, disregarding human commentaries thereon. Proceeding on this thought, it was Alexander who defined faith as the acceptance of testimony ; which, applied to Christianity, involved not, " What do you believe ? " but " In whom do you believe ? " That is, the Gospels endeavour to convince men that Jesus is the Christ. To be convinced of this fact is to be overwhelmed by it. For the issues involved are *personal*—it is a personal conviction regarding an unique Person as the revelation of a Personal God whose love and pardon is for persons who express their faith by a personal surrender of will to the divine Will. Alexander Campbell anticipated by a century the Personalism which has recently become so popular in philosophy. More—he made it the very heart of his religious teaching.

Here again we note the Catholic nature of the Movement. For the essence of Protestantism is, in soteriology, that faith is a miracle produced in an utterly abandoned heart by a special act of the Holy Spirit, unconditioned by the previous disposition of the heart toward God. To Campbell's hard sense, this theology was worse than stupid, it was utterly anti-Christian. But a faith induced by evidence to be weighed by universal reason as a judgment-action at once justifies God in requiring it, and places man under obligations to weigh the evidence and arrive at a decision.

Being now immersed believers, the Campbells were urged to join the Redstone Baptist Association. With considerable hesitation and upon their own terms, reserving the right to co-operate or unite with other Christians, to preach without reference to the Philadelphia Confession, and to denounce denominationalism, they were formally admitted to Baptist fellowship in the autumn of 1813.

So much for the beginnings. It will be observed that those things for which the other five streams had felt and vaguely expressed were gathered up in terms of thinking and explicit statement by this stream initiated by Thomas Campbell. Events now hastened on with more certain steps.

II.—THE CHRISTIAN CONNECTION.

You will recall that we left Stone at the time when Rice Haggard suggested that he call himself Christian only. From the small group left with Stone after this declaration of independence from denominationalism, the next thirty years saw an immense and well-organised church come into being. However, its genius was in some respects quite different from that of the Campbells.

In the *first* place, Stone was a thorough-going Protestant. Thus he accepted without reserve the principle of private judgment. In harmony with this principle, although he himself was immersed in 1807 as a result of his conviction that immersion is clearly taught in the New Testament, he did not require members of the churches to follow this practice. He was content " to let each be persuaded in his own mind." *Again*, Stone accepted without question the Protestant theory of an " invisible church " known only to God. For him the ordinances had little meaning. Baptism was a matter of indifference ; the Lord's Supper was somehow sacred, too sacred to be often observed, but just why he never could determine. He was not troubled about church life and polity, for the real Church was after all invisible. He called his religious followers " The Christian Connection," following Wesley's example. His movement was to be, not a church, but an evangelistic movement of liberal theology and practical moment.

Thirdly, Stone's Protestantism is most noticeable in his soteriology. He and his followers preached against sin rather than answering the question of what to do to be saved. The " seekers " who were convinced of sin, were called to the altar, or mourners' bench, and there they and the faithful prayed that the Holy Spirit might work conversion in their hearts. When the psychological reaction to this painful state of uncertainty had arrived, the seeker was pronounced saved. They were then welcomed into the church, and after this were baptized at some convenient time.

Nevertheless, it would be a mistake to suppose Stone to be an orthodox evangelical. Two considerations involved him in heterodoxy—first, his conviction that Calvinism must be wrong, because it did not work in practical evangelism ; and, second, his intellectual difficulties regarding the doctrine of the Trinity. With regard to the first, Stone became, and his followers also, bitterly scornful of Calvinism. No body of people so utterly discredited Calvinism among the people of the United States as these hardy preachers of the Christian Connection. Most of them had little formal education, but they possessed keen and ready common sense. Their arguments against election would have been buried beneath weighty words in the seminaries ; but their very homeliness carried conviction to the masses. As with Wesley, it seemed never to occur to Stone that his practice at the mourners' bench was inconsistent with his repudiation of Calvin.

And as to the dogma of the Trinity, this particular theological speculation was, at this time, a frequent subject of attacks by

American Deists and Atheists. It was disconcerting to them to find a preacher agreeing that this popular item in symbolics was contrary to reason and to Scripture ! But whatever Stone gained in his conflicts with Deism he lost in his standing among the orthodox. To the clerical mind, if one did not accept the dogma of the Trinity, one must be an Arian—an ecclesiastical fighting word. And since Stone refused to be called an Arian, therefore he must be some kind of a cryptic Arian—and so the more dangerous. The Christian Connection became a despised sect.

This did not, however, damp Stone's zeal. He itinerated constantly. He trained preachers. He organised them and their converts into closely knit Conventions. He instituted a system of circuits. He initiated camp meetings throughout the West. He created in men a fiery zeal for preaching and an intense love of their fellow-men.

The result was, that while the Campbells in about 1820 could count only four churches and less than 200 members who had accepted their reformation, Stone was in fellowship with some 500 churches and 15,000 members. He carried more than one whole Free Baptist Association bodily into the Connection. He planted churches in every settled county in Ohio. He entered Indiana, Illinois, and Missouri simultaneously with the first settlements. He swept Kentucky Presbyterianism largely into his movement. He was equally successful in Tennessee. The only group that maintained itself against him was the Methodists—and they rather maintained themselves *with* him than against him. He drew strength from the eastern movements of Jones and O'Kelly. The phenomenal growth of this undenominational revival movement, much superior in many respects to that of its later imitators, such as Moody's, has yet to be treated adequately by American Church historians. By 1830 Stone was the mentor of some 50,000 people, at least 30,000 of whom were his direct spiritual children.

Two events or movements checked his revival. First, the defection of the Eastern group to Unitarianism ; and, second, the growth of the Christian Baptists or Reformers. We must now return to the latter.

III.—The Reformers (Baptist), 1813-1827.

The outward story of the Campbells as Baptists is soon told. In 1816 Alexander Campbell preached his famous Sermon on the Law. This exposition of Scripture is a practical application of the " covenant theology " of Coccejus, although it is somewhat doubtful how much Campbell owed directly to the Leyden theologian. The principles laid down in this sermon exalt the New Testament as the final Word of God in a long series of progressive revelations. Upon this final Word all perfection is to be built—ecclesiastical, social, and individual. To live by this Word is to be unqualifiedly perfect. To live by anything else, even the Old Testament, is to be imperfect.

The effect of this sermon was to drive Alexander Campbell from the Redstone Association into the adjoining Mahoning Baptist Association. It was perfectly obvious that he was not learning to be a good Baptist. What would become of Calvinism if the Old Testament was to be forsaken as authority? Grateful as we may be to Campbell for liberation from the bondage of the Old Testament, this sermon nevertheless made his name anathema to his immediate Baptist friends.

In 1816 Thomas Campbell formed the acquaintance of one George Forrester, an elder of an Haldanean Scotch Baptist church in Pittsburgh. The aims of Forrester attracted Campbell as much as his legalism repelled him. But the acquaintance ripened into personal friendship. Through Forrester, Campbell met Walter Scott, a recent graduate of Edinburgh, who succeeded to the pastorate of the little church on Forrester's untimely death. This contact was to have momentous consequences, as we shall see.

In 1820 Alexander Campbell was chosen as Baptist champion to meet Mr. John Walker, Presbyterian, at Mount Pleasant, Ohio, on the question of infant baptism. Reluctantly he consented. But the effects were so beneficial to the cause of his reform that he considered proper debating henceforth as one of the most effective avenues of arriving at and exhibiting universal reason on obscure things. He published the debate, which was extensively circulated west of Pittsburgh. For the first time the Reformation had caught the public eye.

In 1823 he created one opportunity and embraced another. The latter was a challenge from the Presbyterians in Kentucky, already hard pressed by Stone, to debate with McCalla at Washington, Kentucky. In this debate Campbell argued against infant baptism on two grounds : the distinction of covenants, Old and New ; and the design of baptism as rendering it inoperative, except to believers who repented and confessed. This debate introduced him to the Kentucky Baptists, as well as to the Christian Connection. To his surprise, he found many among both bodies who heartily endorsed his views. Incidentally, it stiffened the practice of immersion among both Methodists and Christians throughout the West.

27

The created opportunity was the founding of the *Christian Baptist*. He had intended calling his paper *The Christian* but Walter Scott suggested that the addition of the name " Baptist " would disarm prejudice and secure a larger hearing. This paper was iconoclastic. Its leading thesis was " the Restoration of the Ancient Order of Things." Campbell attacked clericalism, legislative synods and associations, missionary societies, Sunday schools, and all " innovations." In all of this he was assisted by Walter Scott ; and their combined work resembles that of the British radical Baptists of the day. But in spite of his agreement with them, there were certain differences, notably the strain of Christian union and the energy with which his views were propagated.

And it is to be further noted that Campbell did not, even in those days of iconoclasm, propose to throw out the baby with the bath-water. Declaiming against theological seminaries, he was at the same time formulating a plan for ministerial education; denouncing Sunday schools, he anticipated modern Christian education methods by pleading for the Bible as a text-book in every grade of public school ; castigating missionary societies, he insisted that the heathen must be evangelised if Christ's Kingdom were to come. His opposition to all these schemes was not altogether the absence of scriptural warrant for their employment—largely it was because of the intensely sectarian spirit which at that time characterised them all. He saw in them more desire to perpetuate the schisms of the Church than to promote the simple Gospel. In denouncing the " clergy " it is to be especially noted that he did not include the Baptist and Independent ministers among that body.* In other words, Campbell in all these matters was a Scotch pragmatist. It was the abuse, not the principle, against which he contended.† The *Christian Baptist* was not, in his own eyes, to be his *magnum opus*. It was to be a preparation for constructive work.

The debates and the paper brought Campbell invitations from Baptists far and near to visit them. It is difficult to over-estimate the value of these tours to the Reformation. In 1824 he toured Kentucky, enlisting the open services of P. S. Fall, leading Baptist minister of Louisville. In 1825 he toured Virginia, meeting Andrew Broaddus and Robert B. Semple, the Baptist leaders of that State. His personal contacts revealed to the Baptists his peculiar charm and godly piety. He disarmed prejudice created by his acrimonious writings. His platform ability rallied the common people to his cause.

* Richardson, *Memoirs of A. Campbell*, vol. II, p. 61.
† *ibid*, vol. II, p. 57.

But this propitious situation was spoiled by his impatience. In 1826 he issued his *Living Oracles*, a revision of the New Testament, in which he combined the labours of Dr. George Campbell on the Gospels, Macknight on the Epistles, and Doddridge on Acts and Revelation. His expectation was that these scholars, being all pædo-Baptists, their concessions to the Baptist position would render their work acceptable to the American Baptists. Consistent where they were not, he rendered *baptizo* as " immerse." He hoped that this version would find hearty reception among the common people, as being a rendering of the Scripture in the vernacular.

But he was over-sanguine. The version pleased nobody. The orthodox of all parties cried loudly against this sacrilege of tampering with the inspiration of King James' version. The masses felt that he had taken their Bible away from them when the old familiar phrases were turned into modern English. And when the Baptists saw their John termed " John the Immerser," their fury exceeded that of the rest. Had Campbell proceeded more cautiously, had he consulted with outstanding Baptist leaders, such as Semple and Broaddus, he might have succeeded. But, for such a work to come unsupported from a reformer, already suspected of heresy, condemned it, usually unread.

Nevertheless, by its very boldness, it appealed to the more independent spirits of all parties. It forced the Church to go behind King James' version to the Greek. Twenty years later the tide for revision was at the flood. While this work, perhaps more than anything else, forced the issue between Campbell and the Baptists of his day, it is to be remembered that it is always the fate of a reformer to sacrifice timid support for the sake of aggressive crusade.

IV.—Independence, 1827-1832.

A year after the publication of the *Living Oracles* we find the Campbells again virtually cut off from communion with all other Christians. The Baptists were consolidating into strict denominational status, which was being retarded by the attacks of the *Christian Baptist*. The people at large seemed unprepared for the New Testament revision. It needed only an occasion to complete the disaffection into open rupture.

This occasion came from an unexpected source. In 1827 Walter Scott became evangelist for the Mahoning Baptist Association in Ohio. His duties were to travel among the churches and hold meetings wherever he could get a hearing. Sitting in the Association were Alexander Campbell and three Christian Connection preachers.

Baptisms reported the previous year totalled only thirty-four for the seventeen churches in the Association. Much concern was expressed at this stagnation. Hence the experiment of an itinerating evangelist. The three Christian Connection preachers commended the idea as already working in their own evangelistic programme.

Scott was now commissioned to this work. But how was he to proceed? He had the zeal for the salvation of men; but he could not imitate the technique of the Methodists or the Christian Connection, and remain consistent to the position which he and the Campbells advocated. In his perplexity he resolved to cut loose entirely from all precedent and discover from the New Testament itself the method of evangelism employed by the Apostles. His study took him to the Acts. He analysed the instances of conversion recorded. He devised a synthesis of these accounts. He arranged the items in logical order. *And then he preached this order, appealing for and expecting response.*

And it came. William Amend, who was too late for the sermon at New Lisbon, heard the appeal : " What must I do to be saved? Repent and be baptized, every one of you, unto the remission of sins, and ye shall receive the gift of the Holy Spirit." This was simple and Scriptural—enough for Amend : he shouldered his way through the crowd, made known his purpose, declared his faith in Christ, and was baptized the same hour of the day.

This is what Walter Scott called " The Gospel Restored." It was a practical application to every-day needs of the reformation urged by the Campbells. It constitutes the chief contribution of the Disciples to practical Christian union. If we become Christians according to the process used in New Testament days, there can be no question of our status. This seemed to be unanswerable. There is no theology involved, necessarily, in this procedure. It is sane and rational. It abolishes the emotionalism which so frequently brings disaster on popular revivalism. It places the responsibility directly on the individual. The Church does not presume to determine the right of the candidate to be baptized. There is no waiting for supernatural manifestation of conversion. Above all, it is a profoundly spiritual process, in that it takes the Word of God at its face value.

This non-theological, rational, ethical, and spiritual method of evangelism has revolutionised mission preaching throughout the whole Church in America. To-day the mourners' bench and the examination of candidates are virtually unknown throughout all denominations, except those with European headquarters. A simple confession of faith in Jesus Christ as Lord is considered sufficient for the laity, at least—and the clergy imply usually nothing more in their subscription to their various creeds.

The effect was electrical throughout the West. Here was a preaching programme that worked. The Baptists in Kentucky adopted Scott's " five finger exercise "—faith, repentance, confession, Baptism, gift of the Holy Spirit—with remarkable success. Elley, Vardeman, and Racoon John Smith each baptized their hundreds the year following. Henley, Ainsley, and Shelburne duplicated the process in Virgina. Scott, in Ohio, found it necessary to call in additional workers to take care of demands from the churches.

The Campbells were sceptical of such success. For eighteen years they had laboured with little tangible results. Had Scott embraced some popular hysteria? Thomas Campbell went to Ohio to investigate. He returned with thanksgiving for the work of Scott. The Campbells had tried to reform the Church by getting it to restore the New Testament order : Scott was restoring the church by building it anew out of the common people—sick of sin, tired of creeds, and anxious to know what God required of them to be saved.

But Campbell pressed on. Leaving Scott and the others to their calling he devoted himself to his study and his editorial office. By 1830 he loosed upon the already weary Baptist leaders two more onslaughts. In January he began a new paper, the *Millennial Harbinger*. The name has been misunderstood, in view of later abuse of the word " millennium " by popular enthusiasts. Campbell chose this name for two reasons : it could not possibly be linked with any sectarian movement of the day ; and it expressed his belief that the Kingdom could come in its fullness only upon the unification of the Church of Christ. Union was not an end, but a means to the culmination of the present age and the total victory of the Kingdom of God over the kingdoms of earth. In spite of such broad purpose the discontinuance of the Christian Baptist led many Baptists to think that Campbell was repudiating them.

Further, in 1830, the Mahoning Baptist Association adopted a resolution, at the instance of Scott, dissolving the body as unscriptural, and meeting again as an Annual Meeting of Disciples of Christ, adjourning *sine die*. Campbell was in the meeting and opposed the proposition ; only Scott prevented him speaking against the motion. For good or ill, the deed was done ; and complete congregationalism was adopted by the Restoration Movement now becoming differentiated from the Baptist churches.

On top of all these—the castigations of the *Christian Baptist ;* the new version of the New Testament ; the new evangelism of Scott ; the new *Millennial Harbinger ;* and the dissolution of the Mahoning Association ; came an action from the Dover Baptist Association of Virginia, under the leadership of Semple and Broaddus. This motion condemned a long list of errors supposed to be held by Campbell, and virtually withdrew fellowship from him and all preachers who held similar views. This is known as the " Dover Anathemas." Adoption or rejection of them became the test of Baptist churches for the next two decades. Theoretically, each Baptist Association was independent of others. Actually, every effort was made to bring all the Associations into line with Dover.

V.—Union of Disciples and the Christian Connection, 1828-35.

Campbell did not wait until driven out of the Baptist camp to promote union with other Christians. In 1824 he formed a warm friendship with Stone. The two men found themselves in essential agreement. To some extent their personalities were complementary. In 1826 Stone began publishing the *Christian Messenger*, declaring his independence of the Eastern section of the Christian Connection. He associated with himself in this enterprise John T. Johnson, the most statesmanlike of the Kentucky Baptist Reformers. These two men began preparing the way for a union of forces. In 1828 Scott and Joseph Gaston joined forces, holding meetings in both Baptist and Christian Connection churches in Ohio. In Indiana, Mathes and Wright joined in fellowship, and influenced Christian Connection churches and Reformers to follow throughout the State. In Tennessee, and in Missouri, the same fusion was taking place.

In these events Campbell saw fulfilled his theory that if union is to come it must be from the bottom, by the people coming together in their local church life, rather than by official resolution of ecclesiastics. Indeed, by 1832, Campbell and Stone would have been forced by circumstances to unite their forces, or each stand in lonesome isolation. Still, some difficulties stood in the way of formal recognition of the union by the leaders.

In the first place, large numbers of the followers of each were not ready for the move. Many of the Christian Connection looked upon Campbell as " all head and no heart," especially in view of his evangelistic programme. Many of the Reformers saw the Christians as " all heart and no head," liable to make unscriptural compromises on many points. Then Campbell still had hopes that the success of the new evangelism amongst the Baptists would overcome the prejudice aroused by his proposed reforms. And in 1832 such a result seemed probable. Thirdly, Stone was not in the Baptist succession, while Campbell was. This consideration did not bulk large with either of them, but it did with many of Campbell's Baptist followers. Fourth, the design of Baptism as presented by Campbell seemed sheer sacramentalism to many of Stone's brethren. Fifth, the two leaders differed widely in their Christology and Pneumatology. Campbell remained a mild Calvinist, while Stone was definitely Socinian on these two points. Finally, Stone's churches admitted the unimmersed to both membership and communion ; while the Reformers, being Baptists, had not considered the question since the formation of the Brush Run Church in 1811.

This looks like a formidable list of difficulties. The resolving of them was preceded by ample discussion and by evangelistic co-operation. Scott's programme of evangelism proved its superiority to that of Stone in actual practice. Thus one of the major troubles disappeared. Theological differences had never been items of communion with either—unity, not conformity, was the ideal of both. Appeal was made to the Bible for the name of the Church and for the design of Baptism. It was agreed to use Scriptural language for Scriptural things. The question of Communion and church membership was to agitate them for some time, but the two leaders agreed : (1) Church membership is secured by adherence to the evangelistic programme outlined in Acts and summarised in Scott's " Gospel Restored." (2) Communion, or participation in the Lord's Supper, is not synonymous with membership, but is an act of worship to be undertaken by individuals on their own responsibility, just as any other act of reverence to and worship of God.

Such were the agreements at Lexington, Kentucky, on the conference between Stone and Johnson and Racoon John Smith, in January, 1832. The results were permanent and decisive in fixing the characteristics of the Reformation, now turned into a Restoration of the Apostolic Church.

It is difficult to determine the statistics of the new forces ; probably we are not far wrong in saying that to the 12,000 Reformers were now added 15,000 Christian Connectionists, agreeing to call themselves indifferently Disciples or Christians. By the union also the fire of Stone's evangelism was added to the logic of Scott's plan. The combination was irresistible. Again, it gave to the new body a conviction that union was possible and certain. Had not Christian union just been demonstrated? Another result is seen in the lessened emphasis by Campbell, from now on, regarding the

33

" ancient order " of church government. This does not mean that he regarded the question as unimportant. But, applying the test of universal reason to this as to all other questions, he felt the conclusions of the Scotch Baptists not warranted, either by the text or precedent of the New Testament, nor by a consensus of scholarship. Finally, the *practice* of theological freedom vindicated the *advocacy* of it on both sides.

The union had no effect in two sections of the country. In New England the Christian Connection had come into virtual agreement with the Unitarians. In the middle Atlantic States the Scotch Baptist influence was strong among the Disciples. But in the section where the two movements were strongest the union was virtually complete by 1835.

CONCLUSION.

Such is the brief outline of the manner in which some six streams of rebellion against denominationalism came together in a powerful Movement to restore New Testament Christianity. The driving motive was an intense longing for the realisation of the Kingdom of God, which they conceived as possible only through the restoration of the Church to the ideal presented in the New Testament. This could only come about through resting absolutely upon the authority of the New Testament, which would produce the unity of all Christians in the mind, and love, and will of Christ as absolute Lord.

Rough Old Racoon John Smith summarised the union well : ". . . certain I am that union with all Christians, on a Scriptural basis, is right ; and it can never be wrong to do what is right." The Reformation of existing denominations had become a Restoration of the Church of Christ.

CHAPTER II.

RESTORATION AT WORK: 1835 TO 1930.

FROM 1835 the Disciples came to stand less for Reformation and more for Restoration. Repudiated by denominations as such, their plea and platform for Christian unity had won approval of large numbers of individual Christians. They had virtually been forced into separate existence. But this separate life had now to be justified. To the casual observer the movement to end denominations had become another denomination. Had it not the usual machinery and distinct self-consciousness? They were thus on the defensive. It had become necessary to define their position before the religious world.

I.—DEFINITION: 1835 TO 1850.

Alexander Campbell's chief service to the Disciples was in this work of definition, to which he devoted himself during these fifteen years. He was now at the height of his powers, mental and physical. None but a giant could have stood the strain of these critical times.

The three major debates of Campbell belong properly to this period. A variation of chronology in the first instance does not vitiate the case.

In the decade of 1825 to 1835 scepticism in America had its climax. Orthodox evangelicalism did not reach the class of thinkers to whom it appealed. Anglicanism and Congregationalism futilely attempted conquest by peaceful penetration. Robert Owen thought the situation ripe for an open conquest of the new republic, and formed his socialistic experiment in New Harmony, Indiana. It was working well. A spirit of defeatism took possession of many Christians.

In 1829 Campbell was induced to accept the challenge of Owen to a debate on the evidences for revealed religion. Owen based his whole case for atheism and hedonism on what he called "the twelve laws": the proposition that man is an animal, everything in his whole constitution being derived from his five senses.

Campbell accepted this thesis, and then demanded: How, then, came the idea of God into the mind? Owen replied, By imagination. Campbell then challenged him to locate imagination within his philosophical system, showing that, according to the

Lockian psychology, imagination is not creative. This argument Owen did not answer ; and, repeated from hundreds of platforms, by local champions of religion throughout the United States, it proved the most effective weapon in the battle against the current scepticism. Not content to rest on this silencing of his opponent, Campbell, in his famous twelve-hour speech, argued that sanity and civilisation themselves depend on a moral universe, and that such a universe demands a moral Personality behind it. Against Owen's fatalism, he appealed to common sense. People have to act as though they had free will, even when they denied it theoretically. But his greatest contribution in the whole of the debate, so far as defining the position of the Disciples was concerned, lay in his discussion of the basis for a sound social order.

Owen assumed that perfect social environment would make happy and good people. This Campbell flatly denied, insisting that society can be improved only through the improvement of the units composing society—individual men and women. No social order is any better than the people who comprise it. And to the end of developing a people of fundamental good will, nothing works except Christianity. The regeneration of men by Christianity is prior and essential to the reconstruction of the social order.

This position found ready acceptance among the Disciples, with the result that they have never been embarrassed by official endorsements of social schemes which have proved unfortunate. They consider the Church has a higher calling than to devote itself either to patching up the present or devising a new social order. At the same time, Campbell made it plain that it is the imperative duty of every Christian to be a superior citizen, judging every social question by the principles of the Christian faith. While he did not expect the unregenerate world to act as though it were Christian, yet he expected a Christian to act as one in all circumstances. The effect has been that it has been rare to find an individual Disciple on the wrong side of a clearly defined social question.

In 1837 Mr. Campbell was forced into a debate with Bishop Purcell, afterwards Archbishop of the Roman Catholic Diocese of Philadelphia. The Roman hierarchy were at the time endeavouring to secure government recognition of their parochial schools. Protestants were retaliating by creating a political anti-Rome party. Mr. Campbell opposed both moves as introductions of the European system into American separation of Church and State. He appealed instead to free and open reason regarding the whole proposition. This thesis he set before the Cincinnati meeting of public school teachers, with the result that a debate was arranged in 1837.

Although placed in the unfortunate necessity of being required to affirm a series of negatives, Campbell succeeded in getting before the public sufficient of the history of the Roman Church to make them cautious about admitting the priests into a share of their government. Although Cincinnati is to-day preponderately Romanist, the city schools are quite distinct from the parochial. His conduct of the debate involved the Bishop in a number of equivocations, notably regarding statements in St. Liguori, which in the public view seemed to sustain Campbell's accusations of Romanists' lack of moral integrity. But his chief attack on Romanism was twofold : (1) that the system involves its devotees in irresponsibility and dependence, which is contrary to the moral ideal of individual responsibility proclaimed in the New Testament ; (2) that the system must be judged not by its professions, nor by its assumed qualities in a Protestant environment, but by its career in the countries in which it has had full sway. It is significant that these two propositions have, since that time, dominated the thinking of American Protestants, as they deal with the political problems occasioned by the Roman Church.

In the Rice debate of 1843, Campbell defended New Testament Christianity against Protestantism. He has been criticised* for devoting two-thirds of his debate to the affirmation that immersion alone is Baptism. This was not due to excessive sacramentalism on his part, for although he elaborated what he called the " design of baptism," as in the McCalla debate, he never did say that there is no salvation without immersion—in spite of efforts to trap him into making this assertion. Campbell is a Catholic, but never a Romanist. Indeed, he actually placed less stress on Baptism than did the current orthodox confessions. But he insisted that if Baptism were of any value at all, that which Christ ordained and the Apostles practised is alone significant. The question is not one of subjective value to the recipient—although experience has its proper place—but rather one of objective submission to Christ's Lordship. And this is a matter to be determined, not by theology, but by linguistics and grammar. Naturally, such an investigation took time. The centre of the whole debate lies in the age-old issue of authority in religion. Have Christians the right to change the ordinances of the Church, or to exercise legislative functions? Campbell made no exceptions to his denial.

In this debate, as never before, it became clear that there is no *logical* ground between Campbell and Rome. Both the Restoration position and the Roman position are logical on their respective

---

* Garrison : *Religion Follows the Frontier*, p. 174.

premises. Protestantism, attempting a *via media*, is involved in inextricable contradictions.

It is to this strain of thought, rather than to any self-righteous exclusivism, that the reluctance of Disciples to accept the status of denominationalism is due. They are, albeit in some cases vaguely, conscious that they think and act in a manner fundamentally different from that of the traditional Protestant. Their outlook is broader than the " branch theory " of the Church.

These three debates gave the approval of all to such public discussions. For full forty years after Campbell's last discussion, Disciples debated with all and sundry. Indeed, there was no better means of propaganda in those days. It was not until 1880 that the daily Press and other methods began to supersede the speaker, in American life. I cannot refrain from mentioning three outstanding debaters of this later period—Henry R. Prichard and O. A. Burgess, and John S. Sweeney. To-day, wherever those men debated, there is a strong Church of Christ. The debates were not mere disputes. They were applications of Campbell's appeal to the common reason of men regarding revelation.

In proclaiming unity in essentials and liberty in non-essentials, the Disciples were following reformers since the days of Meldenius. The difficulty has always been to determine what are essentials. Thomas Campbell early gave a rough and ready formula : " If you will show me how your inquiry affects in any way your eternal salvation I will endeavour to answer your question." Anything later than the New Testament was considered, *ipso facto*, non-essential. Moreover, liberty of thought is essential in the very nature of Christianity. " Ye shall know the truth, and the truth shall make you free." Large liberty of opinion was accordingly posited from the first, as necessary to unity ; although admittedly at the cost of uniformity. Hence the utter repudiation of all human creeds was designed to promote union. Creeds had resulted in divisions : to throw them all over would make the case no worse. Unity, then, is in the faith only. And faith is manifested by simple obedience to the Scriptural teaching, followed by conduct conformed to the Christian ideal. Nothing more than this is required to constitute membership in Christ's body. Nothing more should be demanded by the Church. So, whether one is Calvinist or Arminian really matters nothing. The important thing is to be a Christian. What made Christians in the New Testament will make Christians now. A Christian is one who believes in and loves Christ and obeys Him so far as he knows His will.

The test case came with the accession to the Movement of Aylett Raines, who retained his universalism after entering the

Movement. Universalism was at this time, 1829, widely accepted in the West. It was a reaction against Calvinism. Calvinism is Christianity in a panic of despair. Universalism is the hope that confounds such despair. But it was a terror to the orthodox, whom the Campbells would win. The adherence of Raines brought discredit to the Movement. His right to membership was questioned by the Warren meeting in 1829. Both the Campbells and Scott defended him. So long as a man preaches the Gospel, his private opinions matter not at all. Raines had obeyed the Gospel ; his life was upright. They could ask no more. Raines was approved.

The case is important. There has *never been a heresy trial among the Disciples*—a record unique in Church history. Even the men who have betrayed the faith have been subjected to no discipline, save the termination of their public services at the hands of the Elders of their local churches. No one has ever been excommunicated for his theology or lack of it.

Defections have occurred. Rigdon became the Mormon theologian. Ferguson became a Spiritualist. W. S. Russell in 1860 found no congregation willing to listen to him. R. L. Cave preached his congregation into an adjoining building. E. S. Ames has a congregation, but few disciples. The Disciples are a pragmatic people ; they refuse to take theology very seriously. Every opinion is subjected to two tests : Is it in harmony with the Scripture ? and, Does it square with common sense ? And the verdict is returned, not in a court of law, but in open discussion before all the brethren.

Continuous re-definition of the plea has been made as changing conditions require. Toward the close of the 'sixties Isaac Errett published his *Synopsis*, later expanded into the famous tract, *Our Position*. This was denounced in *Lard's Quarterly* and in the *American Christian Review* as a " creed." But there was no official body to give it symbolic standing, and the cry against it fell unheeded. In succession, Walter Scott published his work *The Messiahship*, Professor Milligan his *Reason and Revelation*, and Professor Everest his *Divine Demonstration*. Lamar added his *First Principles and Perfection*. For the present century Dean F. D. Kershner wrote his *Religion of Christ*. It is significant that no Disciple has written a systematic theology. Books on the position of the Restoration Movement have been helpful—authoritative they have not been. They have won acceptance only as they have contended for liberty in exalting the Lordship of Christ.

II.—Co-operation Achieved, 1850-1875.

With the dissolution of the Baptist Associations in 1830 an era of irresponsible licence arose. Unworthy preachers betrayed churches ; a lack of wide fellowship appeared ; and missions were utterly neglected. Such experience may have been essential in developing the strength of local self-reliance. It likewise fixed in the Disciples a conviction that the unity of the Christian church is to be expressed in faith rather than in uniform service. But it gradually appeared plain that more definite co-operation would be beneficial to the cause at large. The Annual Meetings served as rallying points, but something larger was desired, in view of the national scope of the Movement.

A basis for co-operation had been formed early. The legitimacy of co-operation for evangelism was asserted in a State meeting at New Lisbon, Ohio, in 1831. The *Millennial Harbinger* suggested the county as a co-operative basis in the same year. Rush County, Indiana, put an evangelist in the field in 1833. Ohio experimented in a State-wide mass meeting that same year. Indiana organised the first State Convention and Missionary Society in 1839. By 1850 every State in which there were churches had followed this example.

These State Societies are primarily Missionary Societies. Their membership is generally loose. A Board of Trustees holds the property and employs the executive officers and evangelists. They report to the State Conventions and the general policy is submitted to them for decision. Few of these Conventions are composed of delegates ; most of them are mass meetings. Usually they have a constitution, to which the churches and people generally pay no attention at all. They are interested in the work done, not in the organisation.

As early as 1845 Benjamin Franklin, D. S. Burnet, and Alexander Campbell were all insisting that a General Society should be organised. The question of apostolic authority for such missionary methods was raised. To this Campbell replied in the *Harbinger* : " In all things pertaining to public interest, not of Christian faith, piety, or morality, the Church of Jesus Christ in its aggregate character is left free and unshackled by any apostolic authority."

Acting on this principle, D. S. Burnet in 1845 organised the American Christian Bible Society, to promote dissemination of the Scriptures without comment. After a career of varying fortunes, this society was merged with the Baptist Bible Union. In 1849 the first National Convention met in Cincinnati at the call of D. S. Burnet and John T. Johnson. Summoned as a delegate convention, it found more non-delegates than official representatives present, and solved the difficulty by voting all present as delegates.

The Convention organised the American Christian Missionary Society as a channel for evangelism at home and abroad. Campbell was elected President, and Burnet soon became Secretary. Burnet was a great " starter " of things, but rarely succeeded in carrying projects through to completion. The Society did not prosper. Its first missionary, Dr. Barclay, gave up his post at Jerusalem after four years in 1854. His one accomplishment was the collection of material for his great book, *The City of the Great King*.

General dissatisfaction led in 1869 to the reorganisation of the Society by what was called the " Louisville Plan," designed to placate the critics of organised missionary work. This plan was heartily endorsed by Benjamin Franklin, the leading critic, and he was induced to undertake an executive position within the new society. But the widely heralded plan did not work. Receipts fell off regularly from year to year. Moreover, Franklin and Burnet could not work together. Franklin resigned, and attacked the Society in his paper.

The result was the divorce of the National Convention from the Society. The Convention became known as the General Christian Convention, and was a loosely organised mass meeting. The Society retained its name and functions, but did not plan the Convention meetings. It reported to the Convention, but was not bound by any formal relationship to it.

At this juncture a new voice was raised. Isaac Errett had succeeded, between 1866 and 1874, in building a popular weekly, the *Christian Standard*. His programme insisted that some plan of national evangelism be undertaken. In 1874 Mrs. C. W. Pearre, of Iowa, began a little organisation of women, to study and help foreign missions. Errett's editorial, " Help those women," launched the Christian Women's Board of Missions on its great career. The following year the Foreign Christian Missionary Society was organised. These two societies became popular, and conducted aggressive work. Errett's editorial support, and Archibald McLean's administration and itineration, created a missionary conscience among the Disciples during the succeeding twenty years.

Meanwhile, the American Civil War had been fought. The Protestants of the North had made slavery a question of Church fellowship, with the result that every denomination with churches both above and below the Mason-Dixon line had been divided. These divisions remain to this day. The Disciples were about equally divided by the north and south. What would happen to the churches ? Social leaders were calling for churches to declare the essential immorality of slavery. But the leaders everywhere took the position that slavery was a social institution, and that a Christian's relation to it was a matter of individual conscience. They insisted that the New Testament did not denounce slavery in itself. The evils of the institution were admitted ; but it was insisted that the correction of these evils was a matter for enlightened Christian citizenship not for ecclesiastical resolution. When actual civil war broke upon the country the question was further agitated by the question of the right of a Christian to bear arms. In Missouri the most divided State in the Union, a Pacifist Manifesto was issued by most of the leading preachers, including T. P. Haley and J. W. McGarvey. Some of these men were imprisoned for their act. But Errett and other leaders contended that bearing of arms was again a matter for each to settle for himself. This view largely prevailed.

The result was that the Disciples came through the war united. In 1866 Lard triumphantly headed his leading article in the *Quarterly*, " We Can Never Divide." But it is certain that the war took fearful toll of the Movement. Besides the loss of life, it broke up evangelism in the affected States. In 1860 churches were being rapidly formed southward. From Virginia, Tennessee, and Missouri south into the cotton belt the old battles against entrenched denominationalism were being fought with success. But these States were the theatres of the war. The northern armies swept through them, devastating the country, burning buildings and freeing the negroes. The men were in the Southern armies. All church life lagged ; and the new, struggling churches of the Restoration Movement died at critical points. Church buildings were destroyed. The economic life of the South was destroyed. And when the war ended the men of the Southern armies returned to a barren country and a chaotic society. Most of all, the passions of war and the " subjugation " of the South by the post-war military *regime* created a state of mind in the South which was not favourable to the catholic nature of the Restoration Movement. It was futile to talk of any union, even Christian union, when men were being coerced into political union by the Federal Army. The plea in the South has not yet recovered from the blow of civil war.

While these years were those of the achievement of co-operation this was not accomplished without controversy. Indeed, were not controversy so perennially active among Disciples, we might name this the " age of controversy." Two outstanding controversies were begun in this age, and reached their climax in the following quarter of the century.

The first of these controversies was over the use of the organ in church worship. The question arose in the early 'sixties. Before this time organs were too infrequently met with to cause any question. From both Baptist and Presbyterian connections the Disciples had inherited Calvin's antipathy to the organ. During the eighteenth century the Congregationalists in New England had had a violent controversy over the use of the bass viol in worship. When the Restoration Movement began the people among whom they moved were unused to the instrumental accompaniment in either religious or other meetings, except the fiddle at the dance. It was this Protestant background, and this unsavoury association of the fiddle, that aroused opposition to the use of an instrument as an aid to worship.

But as the amenities of life increased, organs were purchased for the American " parlour " ; and " Music Halls " or " Opera Houses " were built, in which concerts were held, and organs were installed to assist. They proved very popular. America had discovered music.

Led by Isaac Errett, a great body of Disciples seized this new interest in music as a means of enriching the æsthetic side of worship. But the Protestant inheritance was strong. Lard headed the opposition, declaring : " Let no one who takes a letter from one church ever unite with another using an organ. *Rather let him live out of a church than go into such a den.* Let all who oppose the organ withdraw from the church if one is brought in." While some were arguing that the organ is an " expedient " in the same class with buildings and hymnals, others argued that it was both inexpedient and illegitimate : inexpedient, for it hinders singing ; illegitimate for it is not prescribed in the New Testament.

Meanwhile the churches settled the question for themselves in their several congregations. Conventions refused to make the use of the organ a term of co-operation with either the Annual Meeting or the Societies. Resolutions either commending or condemning the organ were ruled out of order. True to their fundamental position, the great body of the people insisted that the question was one to be settled according to the majorities in the several congregations. Its use or disuse could have little bearing on a Christian's eternal destiny. Thus, while many local churches divided over the question and brought the plea for union into disrepute, the Disciples as a whole did not divide on this question during this period.

The other question was that of the legitimacy of the Societies. Disciples have never been in disagreement regarding the necessity of missionary work. They have come to the point of schism over how it is to be done.

The Louisville Plan, mentioned above, failed to unite the forces. There were three groups, each contending for a definite procedure for missionary and all other co-operative service. All agreed that participation should be voluntary. But on what basis? (1) One section of thought, led by Moses Lard, supported by Tolbert Fanning, contended that missionary societies were "innovations" and directly contrary to the evangelistic method ordained in the New Testament. (2) A second school replied that missionary societies were required by the New Testament : that the church is itself a missionary society, and that articulation of its evangelism should be achieved by a representative organisation, each church having an official delegate present at a Convention to which the executive should be responsible. This was Benjamin Franklin's proposal. (3) The third line of thought, represented by Isaac Errett, was impatient of details of co-operation, but intensely interested in results. He insisted that the New Testament made any of the types of co-operation proposed legitimate. That the co-operative work illustrated in the history of the apostolic church was of various patterns. That neither revelation nor the common mind prescribed a uniformity of Christian action in service.

The controversy raged, missions languished, and ill-feeling threatened the unity of the brethren. All three positions could quote Campbell as on their side. But his latest sentiments ; his articles in the *Millennial Harbinger* during the 'forties, when he was in his prime ; and, above all, his example ; all gave the weight of his influence to the last-named of the three. Whether from this fact, or from the inherent temper of pragmatism among the people, this became generally the position of the Disciples by 1875.

Thus was co-operation achieved. Uniformity of work did not come, then or later. But co-operation in one form or another was definitely the criterion of this age. Those who made the most progress in the next age were those who co-operated through Societies. Others experimented with some form of delegate control. Others co-operated through newspapers, such as the *American Christian Review* and the *Gospel Advocate* of Fanning. But they co-operated. The few who did not gradually died out.

III.—INTENSIVE GROWTH, 1875 TO 1900.

These twenty-five years were momentous. They are characterised by bold evangelism, enrichment of church life, serious educational programmes, a vital church press, and the culmination of the old controversies.

There has been a succession of eminent evangelists since 1875. We cannot resist mention of a few—such as the Darsies, the

Sweeneys, Ira Chase, the Vawters, Robert Graham, B. B. Tyler, J. V. Coombs, Wallace Tharp, James Small, Knowles Shaw, Harry G. Knowles, the Brookes brothers, Charles Reign Scoville—but to tell the story of the thousands brought into the churches by these evangelists would be a book in itself. These men no longer relied on preaching alone. They organised parties, with a leader of song and personal workers, to assist. Their work was somewhat similar to that of Moody, but the preaching was more addressed to the reason and the will than was his, and their methods of advertising not so extravagant. Here and there an evangelist would experiment in union meetings ; but the results were generally unsatisfactory to all parties, and it gradually was discarded.

The growth of the Movement is, perhaps, illustrated by a table of statistics—dry as they are. If we assume the number to be about 22,000 in 1832,* which is a most modest figure, equally modest figures follow :

By 1850	..	..	118,000 (three-fold in a decade).
,, 1860	..	..	225,000 (double).
,, 1870	..	..	375,000 (in spite of civil war).
,, 1880	..	..	475,000.
,, 1890	..	..	641,000.
,, 1900	..	..	1,120,000 (fifth among religious bodies in the U.S.A.).

This is the most rapid growth of any religious movement in the whole history of the Church since the apostolic age. When it is remembered that they had no help from emigration, and that only adult conversions are counted, the figures assume new and significant proportions. And when to this is added a knowledge of how careless most of the Disciples were about keeping records, it is all the more remarkable.

From 1870 onward the great westward development of the United States is the most distinguishing social phenomenon. In this expansion the Disciples moved in the van. Their roots are in the first soil turned in the founding of all the new West. This is more significant than at first is apparent, for recent surveys have shown that the life of the churches in America is in their rural membership. Those denominations with a large rural membership are tending to grow more rapidly and display more energy than those of predominantly urban membership. It is now seen that what at one time seemed a mistake of the fathers—to go largely to the country—was after all wisdom, conscious or otherwise.

* Garrison, *op. cit.*, p. 200.

Greater attention began to be paid, also, to the internal corporate life of the local churches. It was demonstrated during these years—and since—that a long ministry has inevitably resulted in a great church. Such men as B. A. Abbott of Baltimore, E. L. Powell of Louisville, I. J. Spencer of Lexington, A. B. Philputt of Indianapolis, Mark Collis of Lexington, F. D. Power of Washington, Z. T. Sweeney of Columbus, Indiana, and later Charles S. Medbury of Des Moines, P. H. Welshimer of Canton, R. H. Miller of Kansas City, and others of equal success, have convinced the Disciples of the value of this means of evangelism. Not only do they preach— these men are first of all organisers. It is they who have provided the executive energy that has systematised the Christian activities of the members of the churches.

But perhaps their greatest service has been to bring a definite challenge to the denominational world in the cities in which they have their homes. Their success is a living demonstration that the New Testament church *can* be restored.

Are the Disciples trusted as citizens ? Judge Black was Attorney-General just prior to the Civil War. R. M. Bishop and M. Y. Cooper were both Governors of Ohio. Drake was Governor of Iowa. They have furnished Governors of Illinois, Kentucky, Oregon, and other States. They have served in both houses of Congress. Champ Clark was for thirty years the leader of the Democratic Party. They have served in the President's Cabinet. General Garfield was elected President. The very nature of their evangelism has drawn to them a body of people not given to uncertainty in either thinking or conduct.

During these years other Societies were added. In 1888 a Board of Church Extension was formed, charged with the administration of funds to be loaned to struggling churches in strategic places. It was a permanent revolving fund. George W. Muckley made it one of the greatest enterprises of the Movement. In 1870 there were 2,300 homeless congregations. To-day there are practically none except the most recently founded churches. This is in a large measure due to this fund.

The National Benevolent Association, founded to care for the aged and orphans ; and the Board of Ministerial Relief, completed the roll of National Societies. But local Societies of all sorts sprang up all over the country. They included societies for hospitalisation, charity, and many other types of service.

In variety of periodical publications the Disciples have, I think, a unique record. This is due to the absence of centralised

For

Honour

and

for

Her!

an Christian Publication Society was
theme to develop co-operation. This
he Christian Age, which claimed to
Pendelton, then editing the *Millennial*
The *Age* had not been created by any
it controlled by them.   The paper
Society.   Four or five great papers
individual enterprise, and with only
could induce by persuasion.   Chief
can Christian Review of Benjamin
of David Lipscomb ; the *Christian*
Christian Standard of Isaac Errett ;
J. H. Garrison. The largest, in point
les, was the *Standard*.

among the Disciples is long and
ents must suffice here.   The earliest
ylvania, made famous by the piety
cGarvey.   The second was Bethany,
largely with his own money.   These
nous during the period of which we
of an immense number.   No one has
a complete list of all the colleges
founded by Disciples.   Wherever there was a new settlement,
Disciples founded schools. Wherever there was a successful preacher,
he would be induced to start a school to train preachers. They have
been in the forefront of every educational advance. Two of their
schools dispute the honour of first introducing full co-education.
Butler University was the first school in the country to place
science on a plane with the arts in the baccalaureate degree. Practically none of the schools were founded by any corporate action of
the churches.   An exception was Butler University, which was
founded through the direct supervision of the Indiana State
Meeting.

Two distinct features of their general curricula may be noted.
First, the colleges were none of them theological seminaries,
although all were founded primarily to train preachers. Campbell's
theory, which dominated their practice, was that to educate in
theology, especially in a separate institution, was to create a clerical
class.   The Disciples would avoid this at all cost.   Second, the
curriculum was always flexible, to accommodate students of every
degree of preparation. Thus, it was easier to gain an education in
the colleges of the Disciples than in the State schools or in the
ordinary church school. Some of the finest evangelists of the
day were the product of the diploma courses, although it was usual
to struggle hard to attain the degree course.

It should be said that two major factors have enabled those colleges which still exist to-day to survive : the generosity of a few men of wealth, and the utter self-sacrifice of the faculties of the institutions. The Churches of Christ as a whole in their corporate capacity have not supported the schools.

By the 'nineties it became apparent that the old controversies on the organ and societies would come as near breaking the unity of Disciples as anything could. The old editors passed. The *Standard* and *Evangelist* remained great papers. But among the conservative papers the leadership fell to Daniel Sommers, who manifested a sectarian spirit in contending for the binding character of opinion hitherto regarded merely as opinions. As a result of his influence churches began to divide over a multitude of trivialities ; and the " conservatives " often were more bitter against their brethren than against " the sects." He did not distinguish between using an organ in worship and subscription to a human creed. The culmination came in 1906, when the United States Census listed the membership under two heads : " Disciples of Christ " and " Churches of Christ."

Nevertheless, the division is not final. Nor, in any real sense, does it exist. It is not a quarrel over faith, but over practice. The essential unity of the Church, as taught in Ephesians, is not broken. There is diversity of practice and service ; there is unity of faith. To see a break-up of the plea in the peculiarities of a few is to disregard that liberty without which there can be only uniformity, not unity. Nor are signs wanting that larger fellowship is coming. Such men as Sommers himself in his latter days, and as George Klingman, are leading the way to a reintegration of the old fellowship.

IV.—To-day's Problems, 1900 to 1930.

It would be presumptuous to speak with great certainty on the past quarter of a century. But I venture to make the following observations :

Organisational life among the Disciples is still in a state of flux. In 1919, after a long agitation, the old National Societies were merged into the United Christian Missionary Society, with a journal known as the *World Call.* The Convention remained a mass meeting. The new Society, under the direction of Dr. Burnham, was a separate corporation, reporting to, but not bound by, the Convention. The expectation was that the unification of the agencies would promote efficiency. But the result has not altogether justified the anticipations. This has been due to two influences : first, the fear that the Society would exercise undue control over the churches ; and, second, the conviction that many of its missionaries and some of its policies were disloyal to the fundamental programme of the Disciples.

When the Society ignored resolutions passed by four successive Conventions calling for a reconstruction of its programme, a number of missionaries withdrew from its support and formed the Christian Restoration Association in 1924. This action, coupled with the declining receipts of the Society, and its enormous indebtedness, has led to conversations looking toward a re-altering of the programme.

The basis of the whole difficulty lies in the small but influential group of men who, lacking suitable educational facilities among the church colleges, went to denominational universities for their post-graduate training. The result was the introduction of Liberal Protestantism into the Movement. They developed a passion for the " social gospel " and a depreciation of the restoration programme. The result has been a decreased emphasis on evangelism and consequent decline in the rate of growth.

But in other respects this movement has had its good side. It stimulated again a definition of the Movement's ideals. Is the programme for the restoration of the New Testament Church tenable in view of to-day's discoveries in the field of Biblical scholarship ? While some have definitely surrendered to Liberal Protestantism others have become convinced that the New Testament is still authoritative in religion. And that conviction has come about by a devotion to scholarship more widespread than at any previous time in the history of the Movement. It has resulted, also in an increased emphasis on the essential fraternity which Christ taught as the distinguishing mark of His people.

The most remarkable characteristic of this age is the growth of education. Assets of the schools have increased from $3,300,000 to $55,000,000 in the quarter century. In 1900 there was no really standard educational institution. Now there are over twenty fully accredited. Of these, five are superior universities. Phillips University, Enid, Okla., is the largest, with some 4,000 students. The College of Religion, at Butler, offers the most extensive graduate training in Christian service.

The controversies of the day centre in the attempted substitution of Liberal Protestantism for the traditional catholicity of the Disciples, and in the dangers inherent in a large organisation which might lead to curtailment of congregational liberty. Propaganda for open membership is loudly heard but largely ignored. The Disciples do not forget that C. C. Morrison, its chief exponent, declared that it was their duty to become a " disappearing brotherhood " ; and that his paper definitely renounced the Movement. In an investigation in 1930 it was discovered that out of 12,000 churches less than a dozen practised open membership.

Despite these problems, in these last thirty years the Disciples have added another 725,000 members. The churches are probably in a better state, generally, to-day than ever before. The quality of preaching is superior. Financial liberality is increasing. Education is forging ahead. There is much questioning and uncertainty, but corresponding determination. The future is difficult but hopeful.

V.—THE IMPACT OF THE DISCIPLES.

Baptists and Disciples have never ceased to regret the quarrel which drove them apart. From the violence of J. B. Jetter's attack in 1857 the Baptists of to-day are as much at variance as the Disciples. To-day little separates the two bodies except denominational organisation. An incident in 1929 is significant. To a resolution from the International Convention of Disciples to the General Baptist Convention, expressing a hope for greater contact between the two bodies, the reply came before the Convention of Baptists from their resolution committee discountenancing closer relationship with the Disciples " so long as they adhere to their traditional doctrine of Baptism for remission of sins." When it was pointed out that this phrase had higher origin than Campbell, the wording was hastily revised. It is to be hoped that the incident will be the turning point, and that union is not far off.

The Disciples to-day see many of their teachings accepted by the American denominations. In 1905 the Federal Council of Churches of Christ was formed, in which Disciples took active part, J. H. Garrison suggesting the name for the new organisation. There is a conscience on Christian unity to-day. There is much confusion as to procedure ; much prejudice ; much opposition, silent but effective, on the part of the officials of denominations. But the sentiment grows. Meanwhile, the Disciples have a programme which is already working, and which will, they are convinced, ultimately prevail. Just how much is due to the Disciples in this development of the ideal of union is for future historians to say. But however the sentiment has come about we rejoice in it.

So far the leading exponents of union place their hope in comity arrangements between the denominations, whereby territorial apportionment is made between the churches. This plan frankly recognises denominationalism as legitimate. Naturally, the Disciples as a rule have refused to enter this scheme. But they have co-operated in so far as they have been permitted to do so without compromise, in other matters, such as general religious and moral enterprises.

A movement of much significance has appeared during the past fifteen years, known as the "Community Church Movement," which is a scheme to unite the religious forces of distinct communities into an unsectarian church. This is a blow at the denominational system as such. But the movement has had no definite plan for union, except to ignore all requirements for church membership other than character—and the character required seems to be ordinary respectability rather than Christian moralism. Nevertheless, its present position approximates to that of Stone's movement in 1832. As such it has the sympathetic encouragement of the Disciples as a rule.

With the single exception of some elements in the last-named movement, no one has seriously attacked the problem of Christian union from the bottom. Hitherto, the denominations have been struggling for a union of sects, which is not Christian union at all as the Restoration Movement has conceived it. The unit in unity is the individual. When the individual is entirely surrendered to the Lordship of Christ, obedient to His will as revealed in the New Testament in express terms or approved precedent, he is one with Christ. And all who are one with Christ are united with each other. This is the philosophy of union to which the Churches of Christ have been committed.

But so far the problem of getting this plea before the Christian world has largely failed. For a time the Association for the Promotion of Christian Unity did good work for this position, but latterly it has accepted the denominational point of view.

Nevertheless, signs are not wanting that this view of unity is coming to be seen by the Christian world. The chief hindrance is the vested interests of denominational endowments, and the prerogatives of official position.

There has been only one force which has made an impact on the consciences of American church leaders as a whole—and that is, evangelism. Converts force attention. The present hour is chiefly hopeful in the increased attention given to evangelism among all sections of Disciples.

CONCLUSION.

Such, briefly and inadequately, is the summary of the history of the six scattered movements to end the curse of schism in the body of Christ by a return to Christianity as it was in the days before schism. I have not done justice to many great men among the American Disciples. I have overlooked many rich anecdotes. I have raced past significant achievements. But such is the price of brevity.

Broadly, the Disciples have stood for five great truths, the impact of which is daily growing in American churches.

(1) They have insisted that the Bible is a book of revelation which is intended to be understood, and therefore possible of being understood, by ordinary scholarship and sanctified common sense. They have made *it*, and not catechisms, the religious book of the people. This does not mean that they have opposed Biblical criticism—quite the contrary. If the New Testament is not true, they want to know it. They have therefore welcomed all light that has come upon the text and its interpretation. But they have consistently drawn the line between discovered facts and theories constructed upon those facts. The significance of these facts has confirmed their confidence in the New Testament as the embodiment of the only norm of Christian faith and practice.

(2) They have insisted that every Christian must believe the Creed of the New Testament—that Jesus is the Christ. They have centered everything in the Lordship of Christ. Theories about his Person have not interested them so much as obedience to His will. The wisdom of this position is being vindicated by both Biblical scholarship and modern philosophy. It is a recognition of Personality as the highest thing we know.

(3) They have insisted that evangelism must be simple and rational, appealing to the whole nature of man, enlisting above everything else his will : that it is in *doing* that emotion and reason find religious synthesis : that to be a Christian is far more than to have an " experience " ; and, on the other hand, that it is far more than ethical perfectionism : that Christ's Lordship is intended to be exercised over every department of life, in the spirit of humility, as His disciples ; and that this submission includes the formal or institutional side of Christianity, as well as its intellectual and volitional sides.

(4) They have insisted that schism is not only unfortunate —that it is sin. Charged with uncharitableness, they have not been able to tear out I Corinthians from their Bibles. They have laid the

responsibility for divisions on the consciences, not on the pocket-books, or on the political expediences or historic witnesses of the Church universal. The sin of the Church has brought it into its present paralytic condition. They have called it to repentance and to first works. They claim, after over a hundred years of experience, that they have demonstrated the practicability of their platform for Christian union. They challenge Christendom to its adoption or to the production of a better plan.

(5) They have insisted that at the bottom the whole disorder in the Church, and failure of its people, is lack of spiritual discernment and life ; and that the essence of spirituality lies not in ecstasy, nor in esoteric formulæ, nor in ineffable self-assurance ; but rather in unification of the whole human personality through devotion to the spiritual realities revealed by the one Person through the ages who has come from the realm of spirit and returned thither to prepare a place for His people. When they have spoken of the inspiration of the New Testament, they have meant that it is the authority of that collection of documents which reveals to man the heavenly things, and how he may attain them. To live by this Sword of the Spirit is to be spiritual.

Such a position is never partisan. It is always free. It is deeply reverent. It is practical. It stakes all upon the essential unity of all life at its best. It is serious. It is joyous. It is humble. It will transform the kingdoms of this world into the Kingdom of God.